IN FOCUS

TRANSGENDER RIGHTS

by Marty Erickson

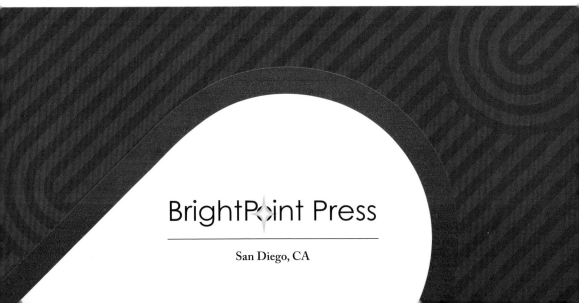

BrightPoint Press

San Diego, CA

BrightPoint Press

© 2020 BrightPoint Press
an imprint of ReferencePoint Press, Inc.
Printed in the United States

For more information, contact:
BrightPoint Press
PO Box 27779
San Diego, CA 92198
www.BrightPointPress.com

LIBRARY OF CONGRESS CATALOGING-IN-PUBLICATION DATA

Names: Erickson, Marty, author.
Title: Transgender rights / Marty Erickson.
Description: San Diego, CA : ReferencePoint Press, [2020] | Series: In focus
    | Includes bibliographical references and index. | Audience: Grades 9-12 |
    Identifiers: LCCN 2019003314 (print) | LCCN 2019005397 (ebook) | ISBN
    9781682827246 (ebook) | ISBN 9781682827239 (hardcover)
Subjects: LCSH: Transgender people--Civil rights--United States--Juvenile
    literature. | Transphobia--United States--Juvenile literature. | Gay
    rights--United States--Juvenile literature.
Classification: LCC HQ77.965.U6 (ebook) | LCC HQ77.965.U6 E75 2020 (print) |
    DDC 323.3/2640973--dc23
LC record available at https://lccn.loc.gov/2019003314

CONTENTS

TIMELINE

1910
The term "transvestite" is used for the first time. It describes people who identify as a gender other than the one assigned to them at birth.

1939
Psychiatrists treat trans people with hormones for the first time.

1977
Renee Richards becomes the first trans tennis player to compete in the US Open.

1900   **1940**   **1950**   **1960**   **1970**

1931
Lili Elbe becomes the first transgender woman to undergo gender-affirming surgery.

1969
Trans women and nonbinary people lead the Stonewall Riots on June 28.

2012
The Equal Employment Opportunity Commission (EEOC) declares that discrimination against a trans person is sex discrimination.

2019
The US Supreme Court upholds President Donald Trump's ban on trans military service members.

1990 **2000** **2010** **2015** **2020**

2014
Laverne Cox is the first trans actress to be featured on the cover of *Time* magazine.

1999
The first Transgender Day of Remembrance is held.

2017
Danica Roem is the first trans woman elected to the US Congress.

THE FIGHT FOR EQUAL RIGHTS

Legal documents usually have two options for **gender**. People can use *M* for male. They can use *F* for female. In October 2017, the governor of California signed a bill into law. This law is the Gender Recognition Act. It offers a third gender option on legal documents. This includes birth certificates and driver's licenses.

Driver's license applications usually only have two gender options: male or female.

This option is described by the letter *X*.

California residents who are **nonbinary**

can use this letter. Nonbinary people do not

identify as either male or female. The law

A person's sex is assigned at birth as either male or female.

also benefits transgender people. They can

change their gender on legal documents.

People are assigned a **sex** at birth.

Doctors assign them as male or female.

This label is based on a person's sex

organs. Some people are born with both male and female features. These people are intersex. Doctors ask parents what sex they want their intersex child to be. Sometimes this matches the child's gender identity. But sometimes it does not.

WHAT IS GENDER?

Gender is a culture's ideas of how people should act based on their sex. Gender identity is a person's sense of gender. Some people identify with the sex assigned to them. People assigned as female feel like women. People assigned as male feel like men. These people are **cisgender**.

Others do not identify with the sex assigned to them. Some identify as the opposite gender. They are transgender, or trans. Others do not identify with any gender. Or they identify with many genders. They are nonbinary.

Laws often ignore trans people. But some lawmakers are trying to change this. California senator Scott Wiener helped write the Gender Recognition Act. He said, "The trans community . . . is under assault in this country. California needs to . . . support the trans community and modernize these laws."[1]

Protests are one way that people fight for transgender rights.

Trans people face discrimination. But many people around the world support them. This includes lawmakers and activists. These supporters are working to help trans people gain equal rights.

CHAPTER ONE

WHAT ARE TRANSGENDER RIGHTS?

Trans people have existed throughout human history. Many cultures celebrate them. They believe gods gave trans people a fluid gender. A fluid gender is one that can change. Many Native American communities believe trans people have a connection to the spiritual world.

Some trans people march in parades to bring attention to their fight for equal rights.

Most scientists agree that gender identity

is broad. It is on a **spectrum**. A spectrum

has two ends. *Man* is on one side.

Woman is on the other. Between these two

The Sex and Gender Spectrum

Sex

Male	Intersex	Female

Gender Identity

Man/Boy	Transgender/Nonbinary/etc.	Woman/Girl

Sex and gender identity are on a spectrum.

points are many gender identities. Gender

identity is personal. It can change often

or not at all. But many people in Western

countries disagree. They have narrow

views of gender. They think people can

only be men or women. This belief is often

influenced by religion. The Bible tells a story

about the creation of humans. In this story, the first people are a man and a woman. Some people think this means there are only two genders.

Western countries colonized other countries. They influenced local cultures. Some cultures became less accepting of trans people over time. For example, British people colonized India in the mid-1800s. They brought with them narrow ideas about gender. A British official enacted a law in 1871. It was called the Criminal Tribes Act. It treated *hijra* people as criminals. Hijras identify with a third gender.

Thousands of people belong to hijra communities in India.

Trans people may fit in this category.

Hijra communities have existed for more

than 4,000 years. They are respected in

the Hindu faith. They perform religious

ceremonies. The Criminal Tribes Act made

Indians less accepting of hijras. Today, hijras face discrimination. Most people do not fully accept them. They are separated from the rest of India's **LGBTQ** community.

LAWS AND OPPOSITION

Throughout much of the 1900s, the term *transgender* did not exist. Other labels were given to people who dressed and lived as the opposite sex. Some were called cross-dressers. Others were called transvestites. The term *transgender* did not exist until 1971. Many trans people were discriminated against. It was hard for them to find jobs. Some trans women became sex workers. They did not have another way to support themselves. Many of them were rejected by their families. They formed communities. They found acceptance in these communities. Violence against sex workers is common. Trans women protected each other. They made sure everyone was safe. Many states and cities had rules against prostitution. Trans women were often arrested.

Many cities also had laws against cross-dressing. One of the earliest of these was a law in Columbus, Ohio. This law was passed in 1848. It made it illegal

LGBTQ people still face high rates of violence. A memorial outside the former Pulse nightclub in Orlando, Florida, remembers the victims of a 2016 shooting. Pulse was a gay nightclub.

to cross-dress in public. More than forty

US cities later enforced cross-dressing

laws. One such law was the three-items

rule. It was enforced in the 1950s

and 1960s. It told people what they were allowed to wear. People had to wear at least three items of clothing from their assigned sex. Trans men had to wear three pieces of women's clothing. Trans women had to wear three pieces of men's clothing. Police officers arrested people who did not follow these rules. Some sexually harassed trans people. They took trans people into bathrooms to check their gender.

THE STONEWALL RIOTS

On June 28, 1969, police raided the Stonewall Inn. This was a gay club in New York City. Police beat up some of the

People march outside the Stonewall Inn in New York City to celebrate trans and gender nonconforming people.

people in the club. They forced people

out of the club. Many people protested

this mistreatment. They staged protests

against the police. Police arrested many

protesters. Some protesters refused to get

into the police cars. They wanted laws to change. They were tired of being mistreated by the police. It was time to make people pay attention.

Cross-dressing laws were eventually overturned. But change was not immediate. New Jersey did not overturn a 1964 cross-dressing law until 2014. Today, people

LAVERNE COX

In 2014, actress Laverne Cox was on the cover of *Time* magazine. Cox is a black trans woman. She gained fame from the Netflix show *Orange Is the New Black*. Cox was the first trans woman to appear on *Time*'s cover. Many people thought this was a step toward equality for trans people.

Trans actress Laverne Cox gave a speech about human rights at the 2019 Women's March in Los Angeles, California.

are no longer arrested for cross-dressing in the United States. But trans people are still harassed because of their appearance.

MOVING FORWARD

It has taken a long time for trans people to be recognized. Equality has not yet been achieved. Society still does not treat

trans people as equals. Each US state

has different laws for legal name changes.

States also have requirements for changing

sex markers on legal documents. Some

CHRISTINE JORGENSEN

Christine Jorgensen was a trans woman. She was raised as George Jorgensen in New York. She fought in World War II (1939–1945). After the war, she read about **hormone** treatments. These treatments were available in Denmark. She moved there and worked with a doctor. Many people told her not to transition. But she went through with the process. She was one of the first Americans to undergo gender-affirming surgery. This surgery changes people's body traits to match their gender identity.

states require letters from doctors and psychologists. Some require medical transitions. A medical transition is a long process. People get hormone treatments. Their bodies go through changes. Some people develop male traits such as facial hair. Others develop female traits such as breasts. Medical transitions also involve surgery to change body traits. They are expensive. Many people cannot afford to transition. Some may not want to go through this process.

Many trans leaders are people of color. They face racial and gender discrimination.

Unisex bathrooms are available to people of any gender.

Violence against trans people is high in the United States. It is also high among people of color. Many activists are speaking out.

They advocate for laws to protect

trans people.

   The first trans-rights groups were formed

in the 1970s. Today they can be found

across the country. Some organizations and

lawyers help defend trans people's rights.

   Trans rights are being addressed in

some parts of society. Some restaurants

and libraries have unisex bathrooms.

Trans people are running for political office.

Some are winning these elections. The road

to equality is long. But progress is slowly

being made.

CHAPTER TWO

WHY ARE TRANSGENDER RIGHTS IMPORTANT?

Public opinion about trans rights is divided in the United States. In 2018, the US government wrote a memo. It said that gender is based on sex organs. It stated that gender could not be changed.

Trans people protested the US government's policies with the hashtag #WontBeErased in 2018.

This definition does not recognize trans

people. Many people were outraged. Trans

people felt the government was trying to

The LGBTQ flag (top) and the transgender flag (bottom) were displayed in a park in West Hollywood, California, in 2018.

erase them. Many responded with the

hashtag #WontBeErased.

Some government policies recognized

trans identities. They protected trans people

in schools and prisons. They also helped

those in homeless shelters. Trans people often face harassment in these places. Donald Trump became US president in 2017. His administration changed many of these policies. This put trans people in danger.

EFFECTS OF DISCRIMINATION

Discrimination is harmful in many ways. Many trans people struggle with depression. They are more likely to attempt suicide than cisgender people. A 2018 survey found that more than half of trans boys attempted suicide. Nearly 30 percent of trans girls said they had attempted suicide.

Trans people attempt suicide for many reasons. Many live in poverty. Some are homeless. Many cannot afford medical care. Others avoid going to the doctor. They fear that doctors will not treat them. This happened to Tanya Walker in 2013. Walker is a trans woman. She went to the emergency room. She was coughing up blood. The doctor kept asking her about her genitals. "It seemed like they weren't going to treat me unless I told them what genitals I had," Walker remembered.[2]

Trans people also face discrimination at work. Bosses may make trans employees

Activists promote acceptance of LGBTQ people in workplaces at a 2017 pride parade.

dress a certain way. Trans people may

have to wear clothing that does not match

their identity. They may be assaulted at

work. This forces them to leave their jobs.

Trans people who cannot find work may

end up in poverty. Then they may become homeless. In this way, it is a cycle.

The trans poverty rate is very high. It is much higher than the overall poverty rate. Trans people of color face the highest rates of poverty. Many turn to sex work to support themselves. This work can be dangerous. Sex workers face violence. They also face sexual assault. Assault cases involving sex workers often go uninvestigated. This is common when the victim is a trans sex worker.

Trans women of color are in the most danger. They are more likely to be murdered

LGBTQ people of color face gender and racial discrimination.

than any other category of people. In 2018, more than twenty trans people were murdered in the United States. Many murders of trans people go unreported. Police sometimes misidentify trans people.

They identify trans women as men. They

identify trans men as women. Police reports

don't use people's real names. Instead they

use birth names. Isa Noyola is the deputy

director of the Transgender Law Center.

She says, "A lot of these [murder] cases

TRANSGENDER DAY OF REMEMBRANCE

Many trans people are killed each year. These murders are called hate crimes. Activists created the Transgender Day of Remembrance (TDOR). On this day, people remember trans people who were killed. The first TDOR vigil was in 1999. Vigils are gatherings to remember people who died. TDOR vigils happen around the world. The names of murdered trans people are often read aloud.

are happening in regions where there are a lack of protections . . . for trans folks."[3] The average lifespan of a trans woman of color is thirty-one years. The national average is seventy-eight years.

TRANS STUDENTS

Many trans students face discrimination. Some schools have policies against this. These policies can protect students from bullying. But each school has different rules. There are no federal guidelines for protecting trans students. In a 2017 survey, 75 percent of trans people said they felt unsafe at school. Many students cannot use the bathroom that matches their gender identity. This also applies to locker rooms.

Some parents oppose trans protections. They think trans people should be identified by their sex at birth. They say they do not want boys changing with their daughters. This argument ignores the fact that trans girls are not boys. Some schools have also barred trans students from playing certain sports.

TITLE IX

A law called Title IX was passed in 1972. It says all students should be allowed to participate in school activities. People

Activists protest for trans bathroom rights in 2017.

cannot be left out due to their sex. It applies

to all schools that receive federal funding.

Many people say ignoring trans students'

rights is a violation of Title IX.

In May 2016, President Barack Obama said gender identity would be protected under Title IX. He said schools should allow trans students to use bathrooms that match their gender identity. Trans students could sue schools that did not allow this. Many people considered this a major victory.

But things changed after Trump's election. Trump and Education Secretary Betsy DeVos took these protections away. The Trump administration reinterpreted Title IX. It said the term *sex* did not include gender identity. In 2018, the Education Department made an announcement. It would no longer

President Donald Trump (left) and Education Secretary Betsy DeVos (right) rolled back protections for trans students.

hear complaints about bathroom rights from trans students.

REGULATION 225

There are many anti-LGBTQ groups. The number of these groups has increased in recent years. In 2006, there were six anti-LGBTQ groups. This number rose to fifty-one in 2017. These groups influence policies. In Delaware, a new rule was proposed in 2018. It would protect trans students. It is called Regulation 225. Many anti-LGBTQ groups protested it. They pressured Delaware's governor.

THE BATHROOM BILL

In 2016, House Bill 2 passed in North Carolina. It was known as the Bathroom Bill. It requires people to use the bathroom that matches their assigned sex. It prevented cities from making their own bathroom policies. Discrimination increased after the bill passed.

The governor weakened the rule. Trans students would need evidence that their parents approve of their gender identity. Schools needed this evidence to protect the students. But many trans people struggle to come out to their parents. Some fear rejection or abuse. If it is passed, this regulation could force students to come out.

CHAPTER THREE

WHO IS WORKING FOR TRANSGENDER RIGHTS?

Trans people face many barriers. Many groups are working to help them. One is the National Center for Transgender Equality (NCTE). It seeks protections for trans people. Trans activists founded the NCTE in 2003. It brings attention to violence

Activists from the American Civil Liberties Union march for LGBTQ rights. They hold signs to honor Edie Windsor, an LGBTQ activist.

against trans people. The NCTE has many programs. Its Trans Legal Services Network offers legal help. Another program is its Racial and Economic Justice Initiative. It addresses challenges that trans people of color face.

OTHER TRANS RIGHTS GROUPS

Another trans rights group is the Sylvia Rivera Law Project. It is named after a trans activist. Sylvia Rivera helped lead the Stonewall Riots. She helped low-income LGBTQ people. She had a difficult life.

INTERSECTIONAL IDENTITIES

The term *intersectionality* was first used in the 1980s. People have many different identities. All of them intersect. People who are from two or more minority groups face many difficulties. They are discriminated against in many ways. A trans woman of color faces more discrimination than a white cisgender woman. Both of them face sexism. But the trans woman also faces racism. She faces gender identity discrimination too.

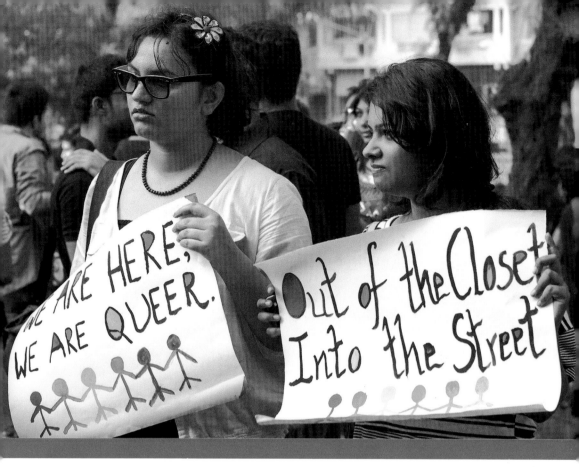

LGBTQ activists protest for their rights in India in 2013.

She was homeless at a young age. She

became a sex worker to survive. She

wanted to help other trans people. She died

in 2002. She was a leading activist of the

LGBTQ rights movement. The Sylvia Rivera

Law Project continues her work. It offers legal services to LGBTQ people.

The American Civil Liberties Union (ACLU) also helps trans people. It has many lawyers. They represent people whose rights have been violated. Some of these cases involve trans people. Lawyers defend their rights in court.

The Human Rights Campaign (HRC) is another major group. It is the largest LGBTQ civil rights group in the United States. It has more than 3 million members. Gay rights activist Steve Endean founded the HRC in 1980. The group originally helped political

An activist supports the rights of trans women at an LGBTQ protest rally in 2016.

candidates who supported gay rights.

Today, its mission has expanded. It spreads

the word about LGBTQ issues.

California Attorney General Xavier Becerra received the Leadership Ally Award in 2018 for his support of LGBTQ rights.

COURT CASES

Court cases have helped bring attention

to discrimination. In 2013, Aimee Stephens

was fired. Stephens was trans. She told her

boss that she was transitioning from male to female. Then her boss fired her. The Equal Employment Opportunity Commission (EEOC) sued Stephens' employer. The EEOC is an organization that protects workers' rights. The EEOC and ACLU helped defend Stephens in court. In March 2018, a federal court ruled in her favor. It found that her employer had discriminated against her.

In 2017, a similar case went to court. Rachel Tudor sued her employer for discrimination. Tudor was a trans professor. She worked at Southeastern Oklahoma

Activists protest North Carolina's House Bill 2, which restricted trans bathroom rights, in 2016.

State University. She had many academic accomplishments. Other professors recommended her for tenure, a promotion. But a university administrator told Tudor she could not apply for tenure. He said Tudor's transition offended his religious beliefs.

He fired Tudor. Tudor won her court case.

She received $1.1 million.

THE EQUALITY ACT

Some lawmakers are working to help trans

people achieve equal rights. No federal laws

protect LGBTQ people from discrimination.

State laws vary. Some states have laws

against gender identity discrimination. But

twenty-six states do not.

The Equality Act was proposed in 2017.

It would be an amendment to the 1964 Civil

Rights Act. It would make gender identity

discrimination illegal. As of 2018, it had not

passed. Lawmakers considered a similar

act in 2013. This was the Employment
Non-Discrimination Act. It passed in the
Senate. But the House of Representatives
did not vote on it.

The 2018 midterm elections brought
the Equality Act back into the public eye.
Democrats regained a majority in the
House. They promised to make the Equality
Act a priority.

SOCIAL EQUALITY

The public's opinion of trans people
has changed in recent years. Much of
that has to do with the media. Positive
representations of minority groups are

Democratic politicians such as Congresswoman Alexandria Ocasio-Cortez hope to pass the Equality Act.

helpful. Trans characters in shows and movies can help educate the public. Trans viewers may identify with these characters. This may help them feel less alone.

GLAAD is an organization that works to improve LGBTQ media representation. In 2018, GLAAD released a report. It found

Trans actress and activist Janet Mock advocates for more representation of trans people in the media.

that about 9 percent of television characters

were LGBTQ. This is the highest number

since GLAAD's first report in 1995. The

number of trans TV characters had also

ACTIVIST JANET MOCK

Janet Mock is a trans woman of color. She is an actress and activist. She is also an author. She has written two books about her gender identity. She grew up in Hawaii. Gender is more fluid there than in other US states. Growing up in this environment helped her embrace her gender identity. In 2018, Mock helped create a TV show called *Pose*. The show's main characters are trans. Mock said, "This is an opportunity to have these people . . . exploring class and gender and sexuality in a way that is accessible."

Quoted in Cynthia Littleton, "Pose Cast, Producers Talk Emotional, Empowering Journey to Make TV History," Variety, *January 5, 2018. www.variety.com.*

increased. Researchers are encouraged

by this.

LGBTQ acceptance groups in schools

can help trans people. These groups are

called Gender and Sexuality Alliances (GSAs). Today, children are coming out as LGBTQ earlier. This may be because of better education. Kids are learning about gender identity. Education may help them express their identities. Diane Ehrensaft is a mental health expert. She works at the Child and Adolescent Gender Center. This center is run by the University of California, San Francisco. Doctors at the center see many young patients. Ehrensaft said,

It's the children who are now leading us. They're coming in and telling us, 'I'm no gender.' Or they're saying,

LGBTQ student alliances help trans people find acceptance and support.

'I identify as gender nonbinary.' Or 'I'm a little bit of this and a little bit of that. I'm a unique gender, I'm transgender.'[4] Societal acceptance of LGBTQ identities may allow youth to be more open about gender identity.

CHAPTER FOUR

WHAT IS THE FUTURE OF TRANSGENDER RIGHTS?

Many people work to help trans people achieve equal rights. Activists believe equality is possible. Many people today accept transgender people. The term *transgender* is becoming more widely used. More people see trans

LGBTQ activists and allies hold signs remembering trans women of color who were murdered.

identities as normal. This is important in the

journey toward equality.

TRANS PEOPLE IN THE MILITARY

Trump promised to protect LGBTQ rights.

Many people hoped he would do so. But he

instead targeted LGBTQ people. Trans

people were especially harmed.

Obama had lifted a ban on trans military service members. This allowed trans people to enlist in the military. The change would start January 1, 2018. But in 2017, Trump reversed this decision. He did not want any trans people to serve in the military.

DON'T ASK, DON'T TELL

In 1993, the "don't ask, don't tell" (DADT) policy became law. It allowed gay people to serve in the military. But they had to keep their sexual identity secret. If they didn't, they could be discharged. Before then, gay people had been banned from the military. Activists criticized DADT. They said it did not promote acceptance. DADT was overturned in 2010.

Activists representing the US Navy march in an LGBTQ pride parade in San Diego, California, in 2017.

His decision was met with criticism. Many judges passed rulings against Trump's ban.

In January 2019, the US Supreme Court upheld Trump's ban. Many trans people

Members of the Swedish military march in a pride parade in 2016. In Sweden, trans people can serve openly in the military.

are not allowed to enlist. This includes

people who have gender dysphoria. Gender

dysphoria is a mental illness. It occurs

when people are uncomfortable with their assigned gender. They experience anxiety and distress. This makes it difficult for them to live normally. It can affect their health. Not all trans people have this disorder. But many do.

In 2016, 8,980 trans people served in the military. Trans people who are in the military can stay. But those who seek to transition could be forced to leave. Trans people are pressured to serve according to their assigned sex. Those who are open about their gender identity could be forced out. Trans activist Charlotte Clymer responded on Twitter. Clymer works for the HRC. She is an army veteran. She said, "I am heartbroken. This is a hateful and cowardly policy."[5] Trans army veteran Evan Young was also devastated. He was interviewed in *Rolling Stone* magazine. He explained why serving openly is important for trans people. He said, "I think serving openly . . . brings people together. When you have people hiding in the closet, it [creates] separation."[6]

PROTECTING TRANS STUDENTS

Being open about gender identity is important. People who have to keep their identities secret may suffer from depression

Some teachers and activists are working to protect LGBTQ students' rights in schools.

or anxiety. This can lead to drug and

alcohol abuse.

Many trans students worry about

rejection. Activists think more schools

need to support trans students. They say

schools need better anti-bullying policies.

Supportive environments are important.

They allow trans students to learn and

feel safe.

Some schools protect trans students'

rights. New Jersey school officials cannot

tell parents about a student's gender

GENDER-NEUTRAL PARENTING

Many parents encourage their kids to have certain interests. These interests may match gender roles. They may encourage daughters to be interested in dolls. Research shows that this is not good for kids. It can put kids at a higher risk for depression and anxiety. Some parents instead raise their kids in a gender-neutral way. They try not to influence their kids' interests. This can be difficult to do. Many toys are marketed to only one gender.

Minnesota trans politician Andrea Jenkins (second from left) works to protect and support trans youth.

identity. This protects trans people's right to choose whether to come out.

GENDER IDENTITIES

Millennials were born between the years 1980 and 1994. The next generation is

Many people are working together today to protect trans people's rights.

called Generation Z. It falls between the

years 1995 and 2015. These generations

have a different concept of gender than

earlier generations. It is a broader view.

About 12 percent of millennials identify as

trans. This is a higher number than the national trans population. Jurgen Maier is the chief executive officer of Siemens. Siemens is a manufacturing company. Maier says that employers should "prepare ourselves for a different future generation."[7] Maier is gay. He struggled to come out to his coworkers. His advice to LGBTQ employees is to "be confident that your difference is your strength."[8]

Trans employees face many obstacles. Some companies are working to address trans rights. The Transgender Legal Defense and Education Fund works with businesses.

Trans actress Alexis Arquette was an activist and icon in the transgender community.

It helps businesses be more inclusive of LGBTQ employees.

Ideas of gender identity are shifting. Science shows that gender is a spectrum. There are many ways to express gender. With activists leading the way, equal rights for trans people may be achievable.

GLOSSARY

cisgender

a person whose assigned sex and gender identity match

gender

a culture's ideas of how people should act based on their sex

hormone

a substance produced within the body that influences how people grow and develop

LGBTQ

a term used to refer to lesbian, gay, bisexual, transgender, and queer people

nonbinary

a person who does not identify as a man or a woman

sex

a label assigned at birth that is based on a person's sex organs

spectrum

an entire range that shows all of the categories of something, such as gender identity

SOURCE NOTES

INTRODUCTION: THE FIGHT FOR EQUAL RIGHTS

1. Quoted in Maggie Astor, "Violence Against Transgender People Is on the Rise, Advocates Say," *New York Times*, November 9, 2017. www.nytimes.com.

CHAPTER TWO: WHY ARE TRANSGENDER RIGHTS IMPORTANT?

2. Quoted in Daniel Trotta, "Transgender Patients Face Fear and Stigma in the Doctor's Office," *Reuters*, September 15, 2016. www.reuters.com.

3. Quoted in Maggie Astor, "Violence Against Transgender People Is on the Rise, Advocates Say."

CHAPTER THREE: WHO IS WORKING FOR TRANSGENDER RIGHTS?

4. Quoted in Sara Solovitch, "When Kids Come in Saying They Are Transgender (or No Gender), These Doctors Try to Help," *Washington Post*, January 21, 2018. www.washingtonpost.com.

CHAPTER FOUR: WHAT IS THE FUTURE OF TRANSGENDER RIGHTS?

5. Quoted in "Trump's Transgender Military Ban Approved by US Supreme Court," *BBC*, January 22, 2019. www.bbc.com.

6. Quoted in Sean Neumann, "A Transgender Veteran's Response to President Trump's Military Ban," *Rolling Stone*, January 23, 2019. www.rollingstone.com.

7. Quoted in "Embracing Difference: Preparing for a Non-Binary Future," *Medium*, May 13, 2018. www.medium.com.

8. Quoted in "Embracing Difference: Preparing for a Non-Binary Future."

FOR FURTHER RESEARCH

BOOKS

Natalie Hyde, *LGBTQ Rights.* New York: Crabtree Publishing, 2018.

Rebecca T. Klein, *Transgender Rights and Protections.* New York: Rosen Publishing, 2017.

Barbra Penne, *Transgender Role Models and Pioneers.* New York: Rosen Publishing, 2017.

INTERNET SOURCES

Denise Grady, "Anatomy Does Not Determine Gender, Experts Say," *New York Times,* October 22, 2018. www.nytimes.com.

Erica L. Green, Katie Benner, and Robert Pear, "'Transgender' Could Be Defined Out of Existence Under Trump Administration," *New York Times*, October 21, 2018. www.nytimes.com.

"Transgender People," *KidsHealth*, January 2014. www.kidshealth.org.

WEBSITES

The American Civil Liberties Union (ACLU)
www.aclu.org

The ACLU works with minority groups. It has resources for trans students and adults dealing with harassment and discrimination.

The Gay, Lesbian and Straight Education Network (GLSEN)
www.glsen.org

GLSEN works with schools to create more inclusive spaces for LGBTQ students. It has resources for Gay-Straight Alliance clubs and teachers.

The Trevor Project
www.thetrevorproject.org

The Trevor Project is a suicide-prevention organization. It has a 24-hour hotline for LGBTQ youth who are struggling with depression or suicidal thoughts.

INDEX

IMAGE CREDITS

ABOUT THE AUTHOR

Marty Erickson is a genderqueer writer living in Minnesota. Marty uses the pronouns "they/them/theirs." They write books for young people full time and like to go hiking.